101 ENTREPRENEURIAL FACTS ABOUT 10 OF THE MOST SUCCESSFUL BILLIONAIRES THAT CAN INSPIRE YOU

What You Can Learn From Their Successes

EF EntrepreneurshipFacts.com

Follow us on social media to stay updated with our new books and increase your knowledge about business and successful people on a daily basis:

Instagram   Facebook   Twitter

Also check out our website for the latest facts and articles about business and entrepreneurship:

www.EntrepreneurshipFacts.com

TABLE OF CONTENTS

Introduction

I want to thank and congratulate you for downloading the ebook "101 Entrepreneurial Facts About 10 of The Most Successful BILLIONAIRES That Can Inspire You- What you can learn from their successes"

You are probably familiar with these names all over business magazines, TV shows, or the Internet.

- Warren Buffett
- Bill gate
- Mark Zuckerberg
- Mark Cuban
- Oprah Winfrey
- Elizabeth Holmes
- Richard Branson
- Jeff Bezos
- Steve Jobs
- Elon Musk

This book is a collection of 101 interesting and fun facts that you might not know about these widely successful entrepreneurs, from their childhood to their personal life, and how they started their businesses.

It is more than just a book of knowledge allowing you to increase what you already know about these famous businessmen, but hopefully it can inspire, motivate and benefit you in one way or another.

Thanks again for downloading this book, I believe you will enjoy it!

Warren Buffett

Quick Facts

Full name: Warren Edward Buffett

Birthday: August 30, 1930

Place of birth: Omaha, Nebraska

Education: Nebraska Lincoln, Columbia University

Net worth: US$66.5 billion (June 2016)

Warren Buffet is a legendary investor and one of the most respected businessmen in the world. He is the chairman, CEO and the largest shareholder of Berkshire Hathaway.

He was born in 1930 in Omaha, and was the second of three children. Buffett is famous for his investing ability. He developed his own investment principles, which has created him a tremendous amount of wealth. Warren Buffet is also known as the "Wizard of Omaha" or "Oracle of Omaha.

As a man with a great heart, he is a respected philanthropist and has pledged to give away the majority of his fortunes to charity.

Fact #1: At age 14, Warren Buffett bought a 40-acre farm with $1,200 of his saving. He made the money from selling chewing gum, Coke bottles, and magazines door to door.

Fact #2: Buffett had accumulated an equivalent of $53,000 in today value when he was just 16.

Buffet's early success with his side entrepreneurial ventures at such a young age made him almost decline his parents' request to go to college because he hardly saw the point of doing so. However, his father overruled him.

Fact #3: According to Warren Buffett, the book that has the biggest impact on his investing philosophy was "The Intelligent Investor" by Benjamin Graham.

It is the best book about investing ever written in his opinion, and Buffett said during one his interviews that the moment he picked up the book was the luckiest moment in his life. That happened when he was 19 years old; the book has changed his life forever.

Fact #4: Many people would think Warren Buffett lives in a mansion, but in reality he lives a very simple life.

Even though he has a net worth of $66.5 billion (June 2016), he still lives in the same small house he bought in 1958 for $31,500. Buffett drives himself without any security and he does not have a cellphone or a computer. He is a fan of ink and paper.

Moreover, Buffett has only sent one email in his life; it was sent to Jeff Raikes of Microsoft. He said it became his first and also the last email when it ended up in court.

Fact #5: If you invested $1000 in Warren Buffett's Berkshire Hathaway stock in 1964, when Buffett took over the company and shares cost just $19, it would be worth over $11.6 million dollars today.

The company averaged an annual growth in book value of 19.7% to its shareholders compared to only 9.8% from the S&P 500. As of 2015, Berkshire Hathaway is the fifth largest public company in the world according to the Forbes Global 2000 list.

Fact #6: Surprisingly, Warren Buffett claimed that Berkshire Hathway was his worse investment ever.

Here is the story. Back then Berkshire Hathway was a textile company that had been going downhill for years. He originally bought stocks in the company with the intention to make a small profit.

Later, Buffett and Berkshire's CEO had a verbal agreement on a tender offer price. But when the official offer arrived in the mail, the CEO's offer price was less than what they had agreed previously.

Buffet got really upset, and he said ego got in his way. He bought the controlling interest in the company just so that he can fire the CEO.

However, Buffett called it a 200-billion-dollar mistake. Instead of investing in the dying textile business, he could have invested in the insurance business, which could produce way better returns for him.

Fact #7: Warren Buffett earned 99% of his wealth after his 50th birthday.

In fact, Buffett's net worth was just roughly $375 million when he was 52. With the power of compound interest, his net worth increased to $620 million a year after, and he became a billionaire at the age of 56 while earning a salary of only $50,000 per year from Berkshire Hathaway.

When Warren Buffet was 59, his net worth was $3.8 billion. That means he has earned over $60 billion after his 60th birthday.

Fact #8: Warren Buffett is one of the most influential philanthropists in the world.

In 2006, Buffett made a commitment to gradually give more than 99% of his Berkshire Hathaway stock to philanthropic foundations during his lifetime or at the time of his death.

In 2010, Bill Gates and Warren Buffett created The Giving Pledge, an organization that inspires affluent individuals to contribute the majority of their wealth to philanthropy.
As of August of 2010, first 40 pledges gave away more than $125 billion combined. On June 2016,

$365 billion has been pledged by over 139 wealthy individuals.

Fact #9: Warren Buffett made an average of $37 million a day or $1.5 million every hour in 2013

Fact #10: Warren Buffett spends 80% of his day reading at the office.

When being asked for advice on how to get smarter during one of his interview, he held up a stacks of paper and said "read 500 pages like this every day. That's how knowledge builds up, like compound interest."

Bill Gates's favorite book "Business Adventures: Twelve Classic Tales from the World of Wall Street," was shared by Warren Buffet. During an interview, Gates stated that it's "the best business book I've ever read." The book was written by John Brook and first published in 1969.

Warren Buffett's famous quotes and advices

"It takes 20 years to build a reputation and five minutes to ruin it. If you think about that, you'll do things differently."

"I always knew I was going to be rich. I don't think I ever doubted it for a minute."

"Honesty is a very expensive gift. Don't expect it from cheap people."

"In the world of business, the people who are most successful are those who are doing what they love."

"Tell me who your heroes are and I'll tell you who you'll turn out to be."

"The most important investment you can make is in yourself."

"Risk comes from not knowing what you're doing."

"It's far better to buy a wonderful company at a fair price than a fair company at a wonderful price."

"If you get to my age in life and nobody thinks well of you, I don't care how big your bank account is, your life is a disaster."

Do you want to know more about Warren Buffett?

Check out our book:

https://www.amazon.com/dp/B01KP852C2

"WARREN BUFFETT- 41 Fascinating Facts about Life & Investing Philosophy: The Lessons From A Legendary Investor"

SPECIAL OFFER!!! Get the paperback version and receive the kindle ebook version ($2.99) for FREE!!!

Bill Gates

Quick Facts

Full name: William Henry Gates III

Birthday: October 28, 1955

Place of birth: Seattle, Washington

Education: Harvard College (no degree), Lakeside School

Net worth: US$76.6 billion (June 2016)

Bill Gates is an American entrepreneur, co-founder of Microsoft Corporation and one of the richest people in the world. Bill Gates was born in 1955. He was first included in the Forbes list of the wealthiest people in 1987 and has been on the list ever since. He has been the world's richest person for 17 of the past 22 years.

His wealth has grown from $40 billion in 2009 to $82 billion in 2014. Gates resigned from being a CEO of Microsoft in 2000. He remained as chairman of the company and created a position called Chief Software Architect for himself.

Today Bill Gates spends most of his time doing philanthropy work. He donates billions of dollars to various causes all over the world through his Bill and Melinda Gates Foundation.

Fact #1: Bill Gates started coding as a teenager at Lakeside Prep School.

The school was one of the few schools in the US that had a computer. The first program Gates coded was a tic-tac-toe game, where player can play against the computer.

Once the school realized how talented Gates was, they allowed him to write a program to schedule students in classes. He altered the code to be placed in classes with cute girls. Gates graduated from Lakeside School with SAT score of 1590 out of 1600.

Fact #2: Bill Gates is a college dropout.

He left Harvard University in 1975 after two years of studies to focus on growing Microsoft. He received an honorary degree from Harvard in 2007.

Fact #3: Gates flew commercial until 1997. He became a billionaire in 1986, which means that as a billionaire he flew coach for 11 years.

Today he owns a Bombardier BD-700 Global Express plane. The plane cost $40 million and seats up to 19 people.

Fact #4: Gates said that he will leave his kids only $10 million each.

He noted that leaving a lot of money to the kids is not a good idea. This first was reported in 2011. In 2014 Gates explained his decision in detail in a 25 minute TED talk he and his wife gave in Vancouver. The entire talk is available on the Internet for free. Here's what Gates said about why he is giving away most of his money:

> "They need to have a sense that their own work is meaningful and important, You've got to make sure they have a sense of their own ability and what they're going to go and do. We want to strike a balance so they have the freedom to do anything but not sort of a lot of money showered on them so that they can go out and do nothing."

Fact #5: Gates doesn't know any languages other than English.

He says that it is his biggest regret in life so far.

Fact #6: Microsoft was not the first joint venture of Bill Gates and Paul Allen.

Their first partnership was the company named Traf-O-Data. The goal of the company was to read raw data from traffic counters and turn it into reports for traffic engineers. Gates and Allen recruited other students to manually process data and transcribe it onto the computer cards. Gates would then use the cards to create traffic flow charts.

Later the state of Washington started offering traffic processing services to cities for free, which eliminated the need for services of Gates' company.

Fact #7: To monitor his employees Bill Gates used to memorize the plate numbers on their cars.

Gates said: "I knew everybody's license plate so I could look out the parking lot and see, you know, when people come in."

He eventually had to give up the habit because his company became too big for it.

Fact #8: Bill Gates reads 50 books a year.

He says that reading remains to be the main source of learning new things for him. His favorite business book is Business Adventures by New Yorker's John Brooks.

Fact #9: In his philanthropy work, Bill Gates was really inspired by David Rockefeller.

In 2010, Bill Gates and Warren Buffett created The Giving Pledge, an organization that inspires affluent individuals to contribute the majority of their wealth to philanthropy.

As of August of 2010 first 40 pledges gave away more than $125 billion combined. On June 2016, $365 billion has been pledged by over 139 wealthy individuals.

Altogether Bill Gates himself has donated over $28 billion to charitable causes, which is the biggest philanthropic donation in the history of mankind.

Fact #10: Bill Gates made a number of erroneous predictions over the years.

He once said that computer users would never need computers with more than 640 kilobytes of memory. He also claimed once that Microsoft would never make a 32-bit operating system. Microsoft rolled out 32 bit Windows NT in 1992.

In a prediction from 2002 Gates said that spam would be eliminated in two years, by 2004. Over a decade later, his prediction still has not come true yet...

Bill Gates' famous quotes and advices

"In three years, every product my company makes will be obsolete. The only question is whether we will make them obsolete or somebody else will."

"I will always choose a lazy person to do a difficult job because a lazy person will find an easy way to do it."

"Success is a lousy teacher. It seduces smart people into thinking they can't lose.

"If you are born poor its not your mistake, But if you die poor its your mistake."

"As we look ahead into the next century, leaders will be those who empower others."

"If you think your teacher is tough, wait 'til you get a boss. He doesn't have tenure."

"Life is not fair, get used to it."

"Your most unhappy customers are your greatest source of learning."

"Be nice to nerds. Chances are you'll end up working for one."

Mark Zuckerberg

Quick Facts

Full name: Mark Elliot Zuckerberg

Birthday: May 14, 1984

Place of birth: White Plains, New York

Education: Harvard University (no degree)

Net worth: US$49.5 billion (June 2016)

Mark Zuckerberg is the chairman, co-founder, and chief executive of Facebook. In June of 2016 his net worth was estimated to be $49.5 billion according to Forbes Magazine.

Zuckerberg launched Facebook with his fellow students Eduardo Saverin, Andrew McCollum, Dustin Moskovitz, and Chris Hughes during their studies at Harvard. Facebook expanded very quickly and in 2012, it had 1 billion users.

In 2012 Zuckerberg announced that he will give most of his money to charities in the spirit of the Giving Pledge. Time Magazine has been naming Zuckerberg as one of the wealthiest and most influential people in the world since 2010.

Fact #1: Both AOL and Microsoft wanted to hire Zuckerberg.

In early 2000s, Zuckerberg created a program named Synapse. The software uses artificial intelligence to learn about user's tastes in music and then recommends songs based on it.

The software had a lot of positive reviews. Both AOL and Microsoft wanted to buy it and tried to hire Zuckerberg, but he refused because he didn't want to drop out of school.

Fact #2: Zuckerberg became world's youngest self-made billionaire at the age of 23.

He had $1 million in the bank at the age of 22, and became a billionaire at 23 thanks to Facebook's IPO.

Fact #3: Facebook's colors are blue and white because Zuckerberg is color-blind.

According to Zuckerberg's profile in the New Yorker magazine, he has red-green color blindness. In the interview he said that blue is the richest color for me — I can see all of blue."

Fact #4: The first website Zuckerberg built had security and privacy issues. Before Facebook, Zuckerberg created a website named Facemash.

The website took photos from facebooks of Harvard's Houses. Users of Facemash could then rate pictures on the grounds of "hotness." The website has a massive pushback. Zuckerberg was banned from access to Harvard's network. He was also accused of violating privacy and breaching security.

Fact #5: Zuckerberg's salary at Facebook is $1.

In most cases $1 salary CEOs receive other forms of compensation such as stock options. In the US such schemes are exempt from payroll taxes. Zuckerberg received a number of other perks from Facebook, too. For example, in 2015 Facebook paid $4.3 million for Mark's security and privacy team. Also in 2015 Zuckerberg has spent over $775,000 using a private jet. This brought his total "other" compensation at Facebook to over $5 million.

Fact #6: Zuckerberg is named as an inventor on about 50 patents.

He filed for his first patent in the summer of 2006. The patent covered a way for Internet users o choose privacy settings. The Patent Office rejected the original patent claim, but Zuckerberg didn't give up and with the help of Facebook's lawyers the patent was approved in 2012.

Fact #7: You can't block Zuckerberg on Facebook.

However, it is not because Zuckerberg programmed Facebook this way. According to Facebook's spokesperson, an algorithm kicks in when too many people try to block one user.

The initial campaign to mass-block Zuckerberg was a result of Facebook's policies in regards to the privacy of its users.

Fact #8: Zuckerberg is the first person under 30 to make one of the largest philanthropic gifts in the US history.

In 2013, Zuckerberg and his wife donated 18 million Facebook shares to the Silicon Valley Community Foundation. The Foundation is the largest community foundation in the world. In 2014 the Foundation distributed more than $450 million to charities in San Francisco Bay Area, US and all over the world.

Fact #9: Mark wears the same gray Facebook T-shirt almost every day.

He says that doing so helps him to save time in the morning because he doesn't have to think about what to wear every day. Here's how he explained it: "I really want to clear my life to make it so that I have to make as few decisions as possible about anything except how to best serve this community."

Fact #10: Zuckerberg spends 50 to 60 hours a week working in the office.

This is very little compared to the average CEO. Zuckerberg says that he likes to take a lot of time to read and spend time thinking by himself. Mark reads a new book every 2 weeks. He reads both fiction and non-fiction. Since his wife is Chinese, in 2010 he decided to learn Mandarin so that he could communicate with his wife's family.

Mark Zuckerberg's famous quotes and advices

"The biggest risk is not taking any risk... In a world that changing really quickly, the only strategy that is guaranteed to fail is not taking risks."

"People don't care about what you say, they care about what you build."

"My goal was never to just create a company. A lot of people misinterpret that, as if I don't care about revenue or profit or any of those things. But what not being just a company means to me is not being just that - building something that actually makes a really big change in the world."

"What really motivates people at Facebook is building stuff that they're proud of."

"Move fast and break things. Unless you are breaking stuff, you are not moving fast enough."

"This is a perverse thing, personally, but I would rather be in the cycle where people are underestimating us. It gives us latitude to go out and make big bets that excite and amaze people."

"A squirrel dying in front of your house may be more relevant to your interests right now than people dying in Africa."

Mark Cuban

Quick Facts

Birthday: July 31, 1958

Place of birth: Pittsburgh, Pennsylvania

Education: University of Pittsburgh, Indiana University, Bloomington

Net worth: US$3.2 billion (June 2016)

Mark Cuban was born in 1958. He is an American businessman and investor. His net worth is estimated at $2.6 billion. Cuban owns NBA's Dallas Mavericks, Magnolia Pictures, and Landmark Theaters. In addition to this Cuban is the chairman of AXS TV, a cable network.

In 2007 Cuban participated in Dancing With The Stars. He didn't win any awards but performed really well for someone who started dancing just seven weeks prior to the beginning of the show. Mark Cuban is also famous for his appearance on Shark Tank.

Fact #1: Cuban's grandfather changed his last name from "Chabenisky" to "Cuban" after landing on Ellis Island.

Cuban grew up in an affluent suburb of Pittsburg, Pennsylvania. His father worked as a car upholsterer and his mom, according to Cuban, had "a different job or different career goal every other week."

Fact #2: Cuban's first business was to sell garbage bags door-to-door at the age of 12 to pay for a pair of expensive basketball sneakers.

He later says in several of his interviews that he learned the fundamentals of business by selling garbage bags to his neighbors.

Fact #3: Cuban paid for college by selling stamps.

His mom introduced him to stamp collecting when he was 16 years old. Cuban says he attended stamp shows just to buy a stamp for 50 cents and walk to the other side to resell that same stamp for $50.

He later chose to go to Kelley School of Business in Indiana because it was the cheapest of all top business schools in the US. This proves that good education doesn't have to be very expensive.

Fact #4: Cuban started a technology company without ever owning a computer.

In 1983, He started MicroSolutions after being fired by his boss after meeting with a client to sign a deal instead of opening the store. The company initially was a software reseller and integrator. In 1990 Cuban sold MicroSolutions to CompuServe, netting around $2 million after taxes from the deal.

Fact #5: Cuban broke a record when he bought his private jet.

He was listed in the Guinness Book of World Records in 1999 as the person who made the largest single e-commerce transaction.
And what did he buy you might ask? He bought his plane over the internet for $40 million.

In an interview with the Wall Street Journal, he later called this purchase a life-changer for providing him with an opportunity to spend more time with his friends and family and get more work done.

Fact #6: Cuban says that Ayn Rand's book The Fountainhead gave him the courage to take risks and taught him about responsibility for his failures and successes. When building his business Mark had a period when he didn't go on vacation for 7 years.

Today Cuban owns a yacht called Fountainhead. The yacht is 288 feet long is 48th largest superyacht in the world. It was built and launched in 2011 by Dutch company Feadship.

Fact #7: Cuban revolutionized the movie business.

In 2004 he purchased a movie studio called Magnolia Pictures and turned it into the biggest independent distribution and production company in the US.

On January 27, 2006, Magnolia pictures released the movie called "Bubble" simultaneously on cable TV, home video, in theaters and available for online streaming. At the time, all experts predicted financial failure for such a move. The movie brought a profit and major movie studios have started to use Cuban's strategy in releasing their indie movies.

Fact #8: Cuban is a book author.

He wrote an ebook called How To Win at the Sport of Business in 2011. To write the book Cuban used blog posts from his website Called Blog Maverick.

In the book, he tells his story about how he started with selling powdered milk and went to selling his company to Yahoo for $5.7 billion.

Fact #9: He accumulated over $1 million in fines from the NBA for different violations.

His largest fine was $500,000 for saying the following about a referee: "Ed Rush might have been a great ref, but I wouldn't hire him to manage a Dairy Queen."

After making this comment Cuban accepted an invitation from Dairy Queen and ran one of its stores for a day. Cuban always donates a matching amount to charity whenever he gets a fine from the NBA.

Fact #10: He is the most famous and most affluent shark on Shark Tank.

The show portrays entrepreneurs making presentations to a panel of investors, who are called the sharks He first appeared on Shark Tank as a guest shark in season 2 and later became a regular. With a net worth of $3.2 billion, Mark Cuban's personal net worth is greater than all of the other Sharks who have appeared on the TV show Shark Tank.

Shark Tank wasn't Cuban's first attempt at reality TV. A few years before Shark Tank Cuban recorded 6 episodes of his own reality TV show called "The Benefactor." The ratings were abysmal and the show was considered to be an unsuccessful rip-off of Donald Trump's "The Apprentice."

Mark Cuban's famous quotes and advices

"It doesn't matter how many times you have failed. You only have to be right once and then everyone can tell you that you are an overnight success."

"It's not about money or connections. It's the willingness to out work and out learn everyone. And if it fails, you learn from what happened and do a better job next time."

"What I've learned is that if you really want to be successful at something, you'll find that you put the time in. You won't just ask somebody if it's a good idea, you'll go figure out if it's a good idea."

"What does it take to be a successful entrepreneur? It takes willingness to learn, to be able to focus, to absorb information, and to always realize that business is a 24/7 job where someone is always out there to kick your ass."

"Always wake up with a smile knowing that today you are going to have fun accomplishing what others are too afraid to do."

"When you've got 10,000 people trying to do the same thing, why would you want to be number 10,001?"

Do you want to know more about Mark Cuban?

Check out our book:

https://www.amazon.com/dp/B01M7MHGLF

MARK CUBAN - Top 15 Secrets To Success In Life & Business: The Sportsmanship Of Business

SPECIAL OFFER!!! Get the paperback version and receive the kindle ebook version ($2.99) for FREE!!!

Oprah Winfrey

Quick Facts

Full name: Oprah Gail Winfrey

Birthday: January 29, 1954

Place of birth: Kosciusko, Mississippi

Education: Tennessee State University

Net worth: US$3.1 billion (June 2016)

Oprah Winfrey is an American media mogul, talk show host, actress, philanthropist, and producer. Her talk show, The Oprah Winfrey Show, was the highest-rated talk show in the history of TV.

She has a net worth of $3.1 billion and has been named the richest African American of the 20th century. Several magazines and rankings call her the most influential woman in the world. In the mid-1990 she changed the focus of her show to books, self-improvement, and spirituality.

Oprah's endorsement of Barack Obama for President of the United States has been estimated to bring Obama over a million votes in 2008 Democratic Primaries.

Fact #1: She had a really rough childhood.

She was born on a rural farm in Mississippi to Vernita Lee and Vernon Winfrey. Her name was Orpah. It was a Biblical name. However, most people were mispronouncing the name as Oprah and later she changed it to the incorrect spelling.

Winfrey's parents were not married. They separated soon after she was born and left Oprah with her maternal grandmother. When she was six, Oprah was sent to join her mother who was living in a Milwaukee ghetto at the time.

Oprah Winfrey grew up in extreme poverty. As a child, she was teased at school for wearing dresses made of potato sacks.

Starting at age 9, Winfrey was sexually abused by several men in her family. Her mother worked a lot of hours and didn't have a lot of time for her children.

Fact #2: She was a very gifted student.

She learned to read at the age of three. She skipped kindergarten and went immediately to the first grade.

She was an honors student at East Nashville High School. Oprah was a part of high school speech team that became second in the US in dramatic interpretation.

Fact #3: She started keeping a daily diary when she was 15.

She called it the journal of gratitude. Every day she would write five things she was grateful for. Oprah said that being aware of those things made her more receptive to good things in her life. Winfrey often encouraged her viewers to keep a similar journal.

Fact #4: Oprah was fired from her first TV job because her superiors told her that she was not fit for TV.

Oprah said that she was absolutely devastated after the fact.

Later she became a host of a failing talk show "People Are Talking." It appeared to be a demotion, but Oprah actually blossomed as never before.

Fact #5: Her show won Daytime Emmy Awards 47 times.

She would have probably won even more awards, but in 2000 Oprah decided to withdraw her show from being considered for future nominations.

Oprah was also nominated for Academy Award for Best Supporting Actress in the movie The Color Purple and Academy Award for the Best Picture, Selma.

Fact #6: Winfrey is a really active philanthropist.

She has donated millions of dollars to multiple charities. She has three non-profits foundations: The Angel Network, The Oprah Winfrey Operating Foundation, and The Oprah Winfrey Foundation.

By 2012 she donated over $400 million to educational charities. As of 2012 Oprah gave out over 400 scholarships to students of Morehouse College in Atlanta.

In 2013 Winfrey made a contribution of $12 million to the Smithsonian's National Museum of African American History and Culture.

Fact #7: Oprah is known for her lavish lifestyle.

She owns a 42-acre estate in Montecito, California. She also has a home in Lavallette, New Jersey, a home on Fisher Island, Florida, an apartment in Chicago, a house in Colorado and properties in Hawaii and Antigua.

Oprah's gardener has spent over five years breeding a new hybrid of roses for the estate's gardens in California. Oprah flies in her own jet. It is a $42 million custom-designed Global Express XRS.

Fact #8: Oprah is the only North American black billionaire and the first African-American to be featured on the cover of Vogue magazine.

Fact #9: In 2013 President Barack Obama awarded Oprah with the Presidential Medal of Freedom. It is the highest civilian award of the United States.

From 1946 to 1961 the medal was awarded to 1 adult per every 86,500 citizens. From 1996 to

2011 the medal was awarded to 1 out of every 20,500,000 adults in the US.

Fact #10: Oprah's interview with Michael Jackson became the 4th most watched TV segment in the history of American television.

With 36 million viewers it was also the most watched interview on TV. Michael Jackson was refusing to give interviews for 14 years prior to talking to Oprah.

The interview happened before the allegations of sexual abuse. The total amount of worldwide viewers was 90 million people.

Oprah Winfrey's famous quotes and advices

"Everybody has a calling. And your real job in life is to figure out as soon as possible what that is, who you were meant to be, and to begin to honor that in the best way possible for yourself."

"Luck is preparation meeting opportunity."

"My philosophy is that not only are you responsible for your life but doing the best at this moment puts you in the best place for the next moment."

"You know you are on the road to success if you would do your job and not be paid for it."

"One of life's greatest risks is never daring to risk."

"Every time you state what you want or believe, you're the first to hear it. It's a message to both you and others about what you think is possible. Don't put a ceiling on yourself."

"The big secret in life is that there is no big secret. Whatever your goal, you can get there if you're willing to work."

"You don't become what you want, you become what you believe."

Bonus - BILLIONAIRES FACT #1

Did you know? In the past 30 years, only 5 people have held the title of richest person on planet: Bill Gates, Carlos Slim, Warren Buffett, Yoshiaki Tsutsumi and Taikichiro Mori. Bill Gates has been the world's richest person for 17 of the past 22 years.

Elizabeth Holmes

Quick Facts

Full name: Elizabeth Anne Holmes

Birthday: Febuary 3, 1984

Marital Status: Single (2016)

Education: Standford University (no degree)

Net worth: US$4.5 billion (2015)

Elizabeth Holmes was born on February 3, 1984. She is the CEO and founder of private blood-test company named Theranos. In 2015 her net worth was estimated to be $4.5 billion. On June 2016, Forbes changed this figure down to zero due to various speculations.

Holmes grew up in Washington, DC. Her father worked for a number of government agencies in the US, China, and Africa. Her mother was a Congressional committee staffer. Holmes was inspired by her parents working in disaster relief and started pursuing science early on in her life.

Her family moved frequently during her childhood, this made it difficult for her to make close friends. Holmes described herself as a "happy loner".

Fact #1: While in high school, Holmes studied three years of college-level Mandarin.
She had a tutor visiting her and her brother every Saturday because her dad did a lot of work in China and wanted his kids to learn the language.

Holmes had a chance to spend some time in China and was really impressed by the Chinese and their pursuit of excellence.

Fact #2: She dropped out of college at the age of 19 because she decided to start her own company.

At the time, she was going to Stanford and studying chemical engineering. One of her former Stanford professors, Channing Robertson, is now employed with Theranos full-time.

Fact #3: The name of Holmes' company, Theranos, is a combination of two words: therapy and diagnose.

The company was first established in Palo Alto. Its original name was Real-Time Cures. Holmes has raised from investors over $700 million by 2015, which valued the company at around $9 billion.

Fact #4: Holmes can't stand needles.

This is what she said in one of her interview:

"I really believe that if we were from another planet and we sat down to put our heads together on torture experiments, the concept of sticking a needle into someone and sucking their blood out would probably qualify as a pretty good one."

Her company has developed blood tests that use just a drop of blood drawn from a pinprick in a finger. The tests can detect a number of medical diseases from cancer to high cholesterol.

Fact #5: In 2015 Holmes' net worth was estimated to be $4.5 billion, but it suddenly dropped down to zero in 2016.

On June 1, 2016, Forbes magazine revised its estimate of Holmes' fortune. According to Forbes, in 2016 Holmes' net worth is equal to zero, based on their new valuation of Theranos to be only $800 million. That means after paying all investors in the company, there will be nothing left for her 50% stake.

Forbes has revised its estimate because it found evidence that Theranos' revenues are less than $100 million and the company has been hit with a number of allegations that its tests are inaccurate.

Fact #6: Holmes's board of advisors includes some of the most accomplished veterans of the corporate world.

One of the interesting facts about Theranos's board of advisors is that there are no women on it. Holmes works with former Secretary of State Henry Kissinger, former Secretary of Defense Bill Perry, former Secretary of State George Schultz, and former senators Sam Nunn and Bill Frist.

Some publications claim that this board was assembled strictly for its political influence. The board does not have any current chief executives from other companies.

Fact #7: She has a vision to change the world at just the age of 9

When Holmes was nine years old, she wrote in a letter to her father saying, "What I really want out of life is to discover something new, something that mankind didn't know was possible to do."

Fact #8: Holmes has lobbied in Arizona supporting a law that allows people to obtain tests without a doctor's prescription.

Theranos's business model, fast results, and cheap prices make it a competitor to Quest Diagnostics and Laboratory Corp. Theranos publishes all its prices. It offers most of its tests at 50% or more below Medicare rates. These two companies are the biggest players in the $75 billion a year US blood-testing market.

Fact #9: Holmes is often compared to Steve Jobs. She likes to wear black turtlenecks just like Jobs did. She said in one of the interviews that she started her business after "thinking about what is the greatest change I could make in the world," which also sounds very similar to what Steve Jobs would say.

Fact #10: Holmes is a vegan. She drinks a mix from kale, cucumber, spinach, parsley, romaine lettuce, and celery several times a day. She doesn't drink any caffeine and limits the amount of time that she sleeps.

Elizabeth Holmes's famous quotes and advices

"I think people can benefit tremendously from really asking why they're doing certain things"

"I don't want to make an incremental change in some technology in my life. I want to create a whole new technology, and one that is aimed at helping humanity at all levels regardless of geography or ethnicity or age or gender."

"What I really want out of life is to discover something new, something mankind didn't know was possible to do."

"At a relatively early age, I began to believe that building a business was perhaps the greatest opportunity for making an impact, because it's a tool for making a change in the world."

"When I thought about having the greatest impact with my life, I thought about all the times people lose loved ones because diseases weren't detected early enough. I thought, 'I can play a role there."

"I think a lot of young people have incredible ideas and incredible insights, but sometimes they wait before they go give their life to something. What I did was just to start a little earlier."

Richard Branson

Quick Facts

Full name: Richard Charles Nicholas Branson

Aka: Old Beardie

Birthday: July 18, 1950

Education: Reed College (no degree)

Net worth: US$5.3 billion (June 2016)

Sir Richard Branson was born on July 18, 1950. He is an English entrepreneur, business magnate, and philanthropist. He is the founder and chairman of Virgin Group, which today includes more than 400 companies.

As of June 2016, Forbes magazine estimated Branson's fortune to be worth US $5.3 billion. Branson is known for his love of adventures. One of his companies is Virgin Galactic, a business that offers space tourism to wealthy individuals.

Fact #1: Branson is dyslexic.

Dyslexia is a reading disorder that results in trouble with reading, difficulty in spelling words, reading quickly and writing.

Despite this fact, when he was a teenager, Branson started a magazine called Student. Branson was really successful at selling ads for the magazine. He talks in detail about the magazine in his autobiography Losing My Virginity.

Fact #2: Sir Richard is a high school dropout.

He left school at the age of 16 to start his first business. He became a millionaire at the age of 23, and a billionaire by the time he turned 41.

Fact #3: Branson initially called his company Virgin because he felt that he was inexperienced at business.

He started the company in 1969 to help fund his magazine. Today the company operates over 400 businesses in over 30 countries, including Virgin Healthcare, Virgin Cars, Virgin Galactic, Virgin Media and others.

In 1979 Branson bought a gay nightclub and operated it until 2003 when he sold it to a private buyer.

Fact #4: Branson owns an island in the British Virgin Islands called Necker Island.

He purchased the island in 1978 for $180,000. Branson was 28 at the time. He started the Virgin

Group just six years prior to buying the island. It was uninhabited at the time.

The asking price for the island was $5 million. Today Necker Island is worth more than $200 million. It operates as a resort and can host up to 28 guests. It is a part of the Virgin Limited Edition portfolio.

Today it is possible to rent the island for $65,000 a day. The Necker Cup is a tennis tournament that is being held on the island every year.

Fact #5: Branson is known as a risk-taker.

He was the first man on the planet to cross the Atlantic and Pacific oceans in a hot-air balloon. He first flew over the Atlantic in 1987. He crossed the Pacific flying from Japan to Arctic Canada and broke his own record in 1991. The average speed during the Pacific flight was 245 miles per hour. Branson invited William Shatner to join him on the first Virgin Galactic flight, the VSS Enterprise.

Fact #6: Branson has been married since 1989.

His first marriage lasted for only 4 years. After that, he married Joan Templeman in 1989 and they have been together ever since.

Branson has a son named Sam and a daughter named Holly. In one of the interviews, Branson confessed that he has lost a child. His first daughter was born prematurely in 1979 and died 4 days after birth.

Fact #7: Branson is a best-selling author.

He released his autobiography, Losing My Virginity, in 1998. The book was then followed by a series of other autobiographical books. Here are some of them:

- Screw It, Let's Do It: Lessons In Life (2006)
- Business Stripped Bare: Adventures of a Global Entrepreneur (2008)
- Like a Virgin: Secrets They Won't Teach You at Business School (2012)
- The Virgin Way: How to Listen, Learn, Laugh and Lead (2014)

- The Virgin Way: Everything I Know about Leadership (2014).

Fact #8: Branson has appeared as a guest on a number of popular TV shows.

These shows include Friends, Only Fools and Horses, The Day Today, The Apprentice, The Rebel Billionaire: Branson's Quest for the Best, Goodness Gracious Me, Tripping Over, Baywatch, and Birds of a Feather.

Fact #9: Branson hosted a contest for his lookalikes.

The competition took place in 2009. It was part of the celebration of Virgin's 25th anniversary. The contest was open to both male and female contestants. The winner received VIP tickets to the anniversary celebrations.

Fact #10: He is against the war on drugs and is really passionate about the issue.

He says that the society needs a different approach to the drug problem and that it needs to prioritize health over jail time.

Branson also believes that money spent on chasing drug offenders and traffickers can be spent much more effectively than it currently is.

Branson is a member of Global Commission on Drug Policy. On Virgin's website, there's a collection of essays called Ending the War on Drugs. The essays discuss the impact of drugs on economies and countries and offer solutions to the problem.

Richard Branson's famous quotes and advices

"As much as you need a strong personality to build a business from scratch, you also must understand the art of delegation. I have to be good at helping people run the individual businesses, and I have to be willing to step back. The company must be set up so it can continue without me."

"Above all, you want to create something you are proud of. That's always been my philosophy of business. I can honestly say that I have never gone into any business purely to make money. If that is the sole motive, then I believe you are better off doing nothing."

"Learn from failure. If you are an entrepreneur and your first venture wasn't a success, welcome to the club!"

"Education doesn't just take place in stuffy classrooms and university buildings, it can happen everywhere, every day to every person."

"You don't learn to walk by following rules. You learn by doing, and by falling over."

"There is no greater thing you can do with your life and your work than follow your passions – in a way that serves the world and you."

Do you want to know more about Richard Branson?

Check out our book:

https://www.amazon.com/dp/B01LY4YHB7

Richard Branson - Top 13 Secrets To Success in Life & Business: A Virgin Entrepreneur

SPECIAL OFFER!!! Get the paperback version and receive the kindle ebook version ($2.99) for FREE!!!

Jeff Bezos

Quick Facts

Full name: Jeffrey Preston Jorgensen

Birthday: January 12, 1964

Place of birth: Albuquerque, New Mexico

Education: Princeton University

Net worth: US$62.3 billion (June 2016)

Jeff Bezos is an American entrepreneur and investor. He is the founder and CEO of Amazon.com. Today Amazon is the largest retailer in the world.

He graduated from Princeton University with a B.Sc. degree in Electrical Engineering and Computer Science. Jeff Bezos worked on Wall Street for a couple years, and became the youngest senior Vice President at the investment firm D.E. Shaw in 1990 at the age of 26. In spite of success, he quitted his job in 1994 to start his own company, Amazon.

Bezos was passionate about space travel since childhood. He is the owner and founder of Blue Origin, a private space travel developer. As of June of 2016 Bezos' net worth is estimated at $62.3 billion, making Bezos the 5th richest person in the world according to Forbes.

Fact #1: Bezos was a very talented child and teenager.

At the age of three, he disassembled his baby crib with a screwdriver because he wanted a bigger bed.

He was a Valedictorian in high school. In one of his high school speeches he talked about "his dream of saving humanity by creating permanent colonies in orbiting space stations while turning the planet into an enormous nature preserve."

Fact #2: Amazon was not Bezos' first choice as a name for his company.

Initially, he wanted to call it Cadabra. Another early name was Relentless. www.Relentless.com redirects to Amazon up to this day.

The Kindle initially had a different name, too. It was first named Fiona, after a character in The Diamond Age by Neal Stephenson, a sci-fi novel about a book of the future.

Fact #3: The first items that Amazon.com sold was a science textbook called "Fluid Concepts & Creative Analogies: Computer Models of the

Fundamental Mechanisms of Thought". This happened in 1995.

In 2015 Amazon surpassed Wal-Mart in market capitalization and became the most valuable retailer in the US.

Fact #4: Jeff Bezos is a big fan of ink and paper.

PowerPoint presentations are banned at Amazon. All meetings at Amazon begin with a silent session of reading for 30 minutes about the subject that will be discussed. This is done to give more power to critical thinking oversimplified numbers.

When it comes to proposals, Bezos requires his employees to write six-page outlines of their ideas and suggestions.

Fact #5: Bezos is a long-term thinker.

One of his projects is to build the Clock Of The Long Now, also known as the 10,000-year clock. It is supposed to be a mechanical clock that will keep time for 10,000 years.

Bezos has donated $42 million to the project. The prototype of the clock is located on Bezos' land in Texas. The final clock will be created in Nevada.

The clock is one of the projects that is supposed to promote long-term thinking. The last update on the clock's website is from 2011. There is no information as to when the clock is going to be finished.

Fact #6: Bezos instituted a policy that every Amazon.com employee must as part of their employment spend two days every two years doing customer service work. This includes Bezos himself.

In addition to this, anyone can email him at jeff@amazon.com. When he thinks that a complaint is valid, he forwards emails to his employees, usually with just one sign added to them – "?"

Fact #7: Bezos is a believer of the "two pizza rule."

The idea behind this rule is very simple: the more people there are on a team, the less productive the team will be. The same applies to meetings. This is why Bezos' rule is: Never have a meeting where two pizzas couldn't feed the entire group.

Fact #8: Jeff Bezos came up with the name Amazon by looking through the A's in a dictionary. He related the world largest river with the world largest bookstore.

Fact #9: Bezos has made a lot of acquisitions over his tenure at Amazon.

The biggest one was the purchase of Zappos.com, an online retailer of shoes for $1.2 billion. The company has also bought IMDB, Audible, and Twitch.

IMDB stands for Internet Movie Database. It contained a lot of information Amazon later used to target customers with certain movie and music preferences.

Audible was a digital audio books provider. Buying it allowed Amazon to extend its audiobook business.

Similarly to Audible, Twitch was a startup known for live streaming. Twitch was working in the niche of video games. Its purchase allowed Amazon to quickly create an in-house gaming studio. Acquiring Twitch allowed Amazon to blend live video, video game and participation experience. In 2015 Twitch had over 100 million visitors per month.

Bezos also bought The Washington Post newspaper in 2013 for $250 million.

Fact #10: Jeff Bezos loves to read! Bezos do not just sell books, but he also reads them. Here are 12 books that Jeff Bezos recommended executives and employees at Amazon to read to help shape the company's culture:

- 'The Remains of the Day' by Kazuo Ishiguro,

- 'Sam Walton: Made in America' by Sam Walton
- 'Memos from the Chairman' by Alan Greenberg
- 'The Mythical Man-Month' by Frederick P. Brooks, Jr.
- 'Built to Last: Successful Habits of Visionary Companies' by Jim Collins
- 'Good to Great: Why Some Companies Make the Leap… and Others Don't' by Jim Collins
- 'Creation: Life and How to Make It' by Steve Grand
- 'The Innovator's Dilemma' by Clayton Christensen
- 'The Goal: A Process of Ongoing Improvement' by Eliyahu Goldratt
- 'Lean Thinking: Banish Waste and Create Wealth in Your Corporation' by James Womack and Daniel Jones
- 'Data-Driven Marketing: The 15 Metrics Everyone in Marketing Should Know' by Mark Jeffery
- 'The Black Swan' by Nassim Taleb

Jeff Bezos' famous quotes and advices

"If you never want to be criticized, for goodness' sake don't do anything new."

"The common question that gets asked in business is, 'why?' That's a good question, but an equally valid question is, 'why not?'"

"I knew that if I failed I wouldn't regret that, but I knew the one thing I might regret is not trying."

"If you think about the long term then you can really make good life decisions that you won't regret later."

"I think one thing I find very motivating — and I think this is probably a very common form of motivation or cause of motivation — is... I love people counting on me, and so, you know, today it's so easy to be motivated, because we have millions of customers counting on us at Amazon.com. We've got thousands of investors counting on us. And we're a team of thousands of employees all counting on each other. That's fun."

"One of the only ways to get out of a tight box is to invent your way out."

"What we need to do is always lean into the future; when the world changes around you and when it changes against you – what used to be a tail wind is now a head wind – you have to lean into that and figure out what to do because complaining isn't a strategy."

Steve Jobs

Quick Facts

Full name: Steven Paul Jobs

Birthday: Febuary 24, 1955

Died: October 5, 2011 (aged 56)

Education: Reed College (no degree)

Net worth: US$10.2 billion (at the time of his death)

Steve Jobs was one of the co-founders of Apple Computer, an entrepreneur, and inventor. He was also a majority stakeholder in Pixar Animation Studios and CEO of NeXT. Jobs is recognized as one of the fathers of modern computers.

Today Apple is the world's biggest technology company by revenue and total assets. At a certain point, the company had more cash in its reserves than the US government. Jobs was fired from Apple in 1985 and came back in 1997. Upon his return, the company was on the verge of bankruptcy.

Jobs worked with British designer Jonathan Ive to create products such as iMac, iPod, and the iPhone. Jobs was diagnosed with pancreatic cancer in 2003. He died of respiratory arrest on October 5, 2011.

Fact #1: Steve Jobs was adopted.

Biologically Steve Jobs was half Syrian. His father was a Syrian Muslim immigrant. The name of Jobs' father was Abdulfattah Jandali. The father objected to the marriage, which is why Jobs was put up for adoption.

The only requirement that Steve's biological parents had was that Steve's adoptive parents have college degrees, with the believe that Steve will later have proper education. However, his mother was disappointed to found out that both of Steve's adoptive parents did not meet the requirement. For the adoption to happen, his new parents had to promise that someday Steve Jobs will go to college.

Fact #2: Just like many other successful founders, Jobs dropped out of college.

He took one semester of classes before dropping out of Reed College. Jobs' GPA during his semester at Reed was really low. It was 2.65. However, he continued to audit classes of his interest for the next 18 months. He took a class about Shakespeare and his poetry and a class in modern dance.

Proably the most important class Steve Jobs took was calligraphy. Later Jobs said that when he was designing the first Macintosh computer he designed all his knowledge of fonts and design into the Mac.

Fact #3: Steve Jobs and Steve Wozniak had a history of working together before starting Apple.

They met when Wozniak was 18 and Jobs was 13. In 1973 Wozniak designed his own version of a classic computer game Pong. Jobs took the game to Atari. The company was a pioneer of computer games and home computers. Atari thought that Jobs created the game and offered him employment, which he accepted.

Fact #4: Steve was a Zen Buddhist and Pescatarian.

In 1974 after quitting his job at Atari Jobs went to India and traveled the country for 7 months.

He was looking for spiritual enlightenment. He meditated often and liked to walk barefoot. He was married to his wife by his guru who was a Zen monk.

Jobs was also a known Pescatarian, meaning that he ate fish but not meat. Pescatarians also eat everything a vegetarian would eat, including milk products and eggs.

Fact #5: Everyone knows two co-founders of Apple, Steve Jobs and Steve Wozniak. Apple actually had a third co-founder, Ronald Wayne.

It was Wayne who created Apples' logo. Wayne has sold his 10% stake in the company for $800 just two weeks after partnering with Jobs and Wozniak. Today his stake could have been worth around $60 billion.

Fact #6: The reason why Jobs named his company Apple was very simple: it was the word that came before Atari in the phone book.

This happened before the invention of the Internet, when a lot of people used alphabetically structured phone books and printed directories to look for products and services.

Jobs was employed at Atari before starting Apple and needed to come up with a name before 5pm on that day. Before getting a job at Atari Jobs actually worked on an apple farm in Oregon.

Fact #7: Jobs used to take drugs and said that taking LSD was "one of the two or three most important things I have done in my life."

He claimed that LSD helped him to "think differently." "Think differently" was a slogan of Apple for many years.

Fact #8: Jobs refused to give money to charity.

When he became the CEO of Apple, he stopped the company's participation in all charitable activities saying that they had to "wait until we are profitable."

However, after his death, the current Apple CEO Tim Cook has publicly announced several of number of private philanthropic efforts undertaken by Jobs during his life.

Fact #9: Jobs didn't like to fire people, especially after he had kids of his own.

Here's what he said: "When I look at people when this happens, I also think of them as being 5 years old, kind of like I look at my kids. And I think that that could be me coming home to tell my wife and kids that I just got laid off. Or that it could be one of my kids in 20 years. I never took it so personally before."

Fact #10: Jobs turned down a liver transplant offer from Tim Cook.

The next CEO of Apple and Jobs were so close that Cook offered a portion of his liver when he learned that Jobs was sick. Jobs refused the offer right after Cook made the suggestion.

Steve Jobs' famous quotes and advices

"Being the richest man in the cemetery doesn't matter to me. Going to bed at night saying we've done something wonderful...that's what matters to me."

"The people who are crazy enough to think they can change the world are the ones who do."

"Your time is limited, so don't waste it living someone else's life. Don't be trapped by dogma—which is living with the results of other people's thinking. Don't let the noise of others' opinions drown out your own inner voice. And most important, have the courage to follow your heart and intuition."

"For the past 33 years, I have looked in the mirror every morning and asked myself: 'If today were the last day of my life, would I want to do what I am about to do today?' And whenever the answer has been 'No' for too many days in a row, I know I need to change something."

"The only way to do great work is to love what you do. If you haven't found it yet, keep looking. Don't settle. As with all matters of the heart, you'll know when you've found it."

"If you are working on something exciting that you really care about, you don't have to be pushed. The vision pulls you."

Do you want to know more about Steve Jobs?

Check out our book:

https://www.amazon.com/dp/B01LYICYK4

Steve Jobs - Top 13 Secrets To Success in Life & Business: The Power Of Think Different

SPECIAL OFFER!!! Get the paperback version and receive the kindle ebook version ($2.99) for FREE!!!

Elon Musk

Quick Facts

Full name: Elon Reeve Musk

Birthday: June 28, 1971

Place of birth: Pretoria, Transvaal, South Africa

Education: University of Pennsylvania

Net worth: US$12.6 billion (June 2016)

Elon Musk is a Canadian-American entrepreneur, scientist, inventor an engineer. He is considered as one of the greatest and most prolific modern inventors. Elon Musk is responsible for monumental advancements in futuristic technology like renewable energy and space travel.

Musk is the founder and CEO of SpaceX, with the vision to expand life to other planets, CEO of Tesla Motors, co-founder and chairman of SolarCity.

As of June of 2016 his net worth was estimated to be $12.6 billion, making Musk the 94th wealthiest person in the world. All Musk's companies and goals revolve around his vision to improve the world and change the way people live their lives.

Fact #1: Elon Musk was born is South Africa in 1971. Just like Bill Gates, he was interested in coding from an early age. He created and sold his first software at the age of 12. It was a computer game called Blaster. A web version of the game is available online to this day.

Fact #2: Musk has moved to California to go to Stanford after receiving a degree from University of Pennsylvania.

Musk dropped out of Stanford just two days after enrollment because he decided to focus on making money during the Internet boom. His first company, Zip2, was established shortly thereafter.

Fact #3: Musk became a millionaire at the age of 28.

1995 Musk and his brother Kimbal started Zip2. The company was started with $28,000 the brothers loaned from their father.

The company represented Elon's vision of Yellow Pages on the Internet: Zip2 created an Internet "city guide" originally available in the Bay Area.

Musk pitched the services of the company door-to-door together with brother and a team of salespeople he hired. Later the brothers were able to get contracts with The New York Times and Chicago Tribune.

Compaq bought Zip2 in the February of 1999 for $307 million in cash and $34 million in stock options. Elon owned 7% of the company, which resulted in him getting $22 million from the sale.

Zip2 became a part of MyWay.com, which ceased to exist in 2002. However, the technology was purchased by BellSouth for its consumer portal.

Fact #4: Elon Musk didn't like his kids' school, so he just opened his own.

The school is called Ad Astra, which means "To the stars." It is relative secret without much information about the school available online; and the school only has about 20 kids as of September 2015.

Musk's vision of the school is removing grade levels so that there would be no differentiation between a first grader and a third grader.

"Some people love English or languages. Some people love math. Some people love music. Different abilities, different times," he says. "It makes more sense to cater the education to match their aptitudes and abilities."

Fact #5: With $10 million from the Zip2 sale, in 1999 Musk cofounded X.com, a payment company that later became PayPal.

In the first years of its existence, PayPal had 7-10% daily growth thanks to its referral program. After the first month of operations, PayPal had 100,000 members.

The company would offer people $20 to open an account and $20 per referral. Musk has spent around $60 million on this kind of marketing.

In 2002 the company was acquired by eBay for 1.5 billion, of which Musk received $165 million.

Fact #6: Musk founded Space X, also known as Space Exploration Technologies, in 2002 with $100 million of his own money.

The goal of the company is to expand human life beyond Earth. He created the company after traveling to Russia and trying to buy refurbished space launch vehicles there.

Initially, Musk couldn't get any outside funding for SpaceX because investors thought that the company was just a crazy dream.

In September 2009 SpaceX launched Falcon 1 rocket, which sent a satellite into the orbit of the Earth; and SpaceX became the first private company to do so. Today Space X is the largest private manufacturer of rocket motors in the world.

When people ask Musk as to why he decided to create SpaceX, he would reply with his punchline: "People would say, "Did you hear the joke about the guy who made a small fortune in the space industry?" Obviously, "He started with a large one." And so I tell people, well, I was trying to figure out the fastest way to turn a large fortune into a small one. And they'd look at me, like, "Is he serious?"

Speaking seriously, Musk feels that SpaceX is about long-term innovation and he's not particularly worried about it not making money in the short run.

Fact #7: Musk created Tesla in 2003, which focus on developing electric cars.

Tesla Model S received 5.4 out of 5 safety rating from the National Highway Safety Administration. This was the highest safety rating ever issued to a car.

After the introduction of the Model 3 in early 2016, Tesla received 276,000 preorders with $1000 deposit for each in just 72 hours.

Fact #8: Musk was the author of the concept and investor into SolarCity, a company co-founded by his cousins.

The mission of the company is "to make a big difference in the fight against climate change."

Today Musk remains the largest shareholder in the company. SolarCity is the second largest provider of solar power in the US.

Fact #9: Musk's official salary at Tesla Motors is just $1.

Some wealthy CEOs get paid mostly in "additional benefits" and stock options for tax purposes. Musk is one of them. By 2022 he is supposed to get $1.6 billion in stock options. The pay structure is strictly related to Tesla's stock performance. Every time Tesla's valuation goes up $4 billion up to $43.2 billion, Musk gets a 10% bonus in options. There are also three milestones. They include the company selling 100,000, 200,000 and 300,000 vehicles. By the end of 2015 the company has sold 107,000 cars, so Musk is on target to accomplish the goal.

Fact #10: While starting Zip2, Elon Musk and his brother didn't have enough money for rent, so they had to sleep in the office and go to YMCA for shower.

During an interview, Musk says "When you are first starting out you really need to make your burn-rate ridiculously tiny. Don't spend more than you are sure you have."

Fact #11: Elon Musk is viewed as real life super hero, dedicated to providing worldwide solutions to international problems.

He was the inspiration for the film depiction of genius billionaire Tony Stark in Iron Man movies. Parts of Iron Man 2 were filmed at SpaceX, and Musk also appeared in a short scene.

Musk also named one of his sons, Xavier, after Professor Xavier of X-Men.

Elon Musk's famous quotes and advices

"You want to do projects that are inspiring and make people excited about the future. Life has to be about more than just solving problems…"

"The first step is to establish that something is possible; then probability will occur."

"My biggest mistake is probably weighing too much on someone's talent and not someone's personality. I think it matters whether someone has a good heart."

"I think it is possible for ordinary people to choose to be extraordinary."

"Going from PayPal, I thought: 'Well, what are some of the other problems that are likely to most affect the future of humanity?' Not from the perspective, 'What's the best way to make money?"

"If you go back a few hundred years, what we take for granted today would seem like magic – being able to talk to people over long distances, to transmit images, flying, accessing vast amounts of data like an oracle. These are all things that would have been considered magic a few hundred years ago."

"When I was in college, I wanted to be involved in things that would change the world. Now I am."

Do you want to know more about Elon Musk?

Check out our book:

https://www.amazon.com/dp/B01LIUK5DW

Elon Musk - Top 10 Business Lessons Through An Inspiring Life Of A Visionary Entrepreneur: The Man With A Quest To Change The World's Future

SPECIAL OFFER!!! Get the paperback version and receive the kindle ebook version ($2.99) for FREE!!!

Bonus - BILLIONAIRES FACT #2

Did you know? The first confirmed U.S. dollar billionaire was the American oil magnate John D. Rockefeller, back in the 1916. By the time Rockefeller died in 1937, his assets equaled 1.5% of America's total economic output. Bill Gates has about .38% today.

Conclusion

Congratulations! Thank you again for purchasing this book and having read it this far!

One thing that most of these successful entrepreneurs have in common is that they constantly update themselves with new knowledge through reading- just like Warren Buffet's famous quote "The best investment you can make is in yourself."

I hope you enjoyed reading this book "101 Entrepreneurial Facts About 10 of The Most Successful BILLIONAIRES That Can Inspire You- What you can learn from their successes" and were able to take something out of these facts that considered as valuable.

I wish you the best of luck, and hopefully one day you will be like these successful entrepreneurs.

Entrepreneurship Facts.

Finally, if you enjoyed this book, then I'd like to ask you for a favor, would you be kind enough to leave a review for this book on Amazon? Tell us what you like or dislike and what we can improve. Your feedbacks will be greatly appreciated!

https://www.amazon.com/dp/B01HK0B22C

Follow us on social media to stay updated with our new books and increase your entrepreneurial knowledge on a daily basis:

Instagram   Facebook   Twitter

Check out our website for the latest facts and articles about business and entrepreneurship:

www.EntrepreneurshipFacts.com

More books by Entrepreneurship Facts

101 Fascinating Facts About 10 Of The Most Recognizable Companies In The World

The Real Life RICH DAD & The Lessons He Taught ROBERT KIYOSAKI about Money

Images Credit

Bill Gates
https://commons.wikimedia.org/wiki/File:Bill_Gates_July_2014.jpg

Warren Buffett
https://en.wikipedia.org/wiki/Warren_Buffett#/media/File:Warren_Buffett_KU_Visit.jpg

Mark Zuckerberg
https://www.flickr.com/photos/deneyterrio/2321206299

Mark Cuban
https://www.flickr.com/photos/keithallison/3126421377

Oprah Winfrey
https://www.flickr.com/photos/aphrodite-in-nyc/15445694840

Elizabeth Holmes
https://www.flickr.com/photos/techcrunch/14996937900

Jeff Bezos
https://commons.wikimedia.org/wiki/File:Jeff_Bezos%27_iconic_laugh_crop.jpg

Steve Jobs
https://commons.wikimedia.org/wiki/File:Steve_Jobs_Headshot_2010-CROP.jpg

Elon Musk
https://www.flickr.com/photos/jurvetson/18659265152/